Stays the Heart

poems by

Emily Pulfer-Terino

Finishing Line Press
Georgetown, Kentucky

Stays the Heart

Copyright © 2016 by Emily Pulfer-Terino
ISBN 978-1-944251-28-4 First Edition
All rights reserved under International and Pan-American Copyright Conventions.
No part of this book may be reproduced in any manner whatsoever without written
permission from the publisher, except in the case of brief quotations embodied in critical
articles and reviews.

ACKNOWLEDGMENTS

"Pawnshop", forthcoming in *Dogwood*
"Cliff Dwellings, Mesa Verde"—published in T*upelo Quarterly*
"Storm"—forthcoming in *Stone Canoe*
"Tinctures"—published in *Numero Cinq Magazine*
"What Will Never Be"— published in *The Southeast Review*

Editor: Christen Kincaid

Cover Art: Theodore Pulfer-Terino

Author Photo: Anne Rubin

Cover Design: Elizabeth Maines

Printed in the USA on acid-free paper.
Order online: www.finishinglinepress.com
        also available on amazon.com

                Author inquiries and mail orders:
                     Finishing Line Press
                        P. O. Box 1626
                 Georgetown, Kentucky 40324
                           U. S. A.

Table of Contents

I

What Will Never Be 1

In Spring 3

Postscript 4

Storm 5

Pawnshop 6

Cliff Dwellings, Mesa Verde 7

II

Tinctures 11

Apples 12

Aubade 13

North Street 14

Dogwood 15

III

Nest 19

Fall 20

My Mother's Patent Leather Pumps 21

Elegy For My Mother's Dress 22

Lilacs 23

The Garden 25

*Just now, as we meet again, the season of falling
Blossoms gracing this world—how lovely it is.*

Tu Fu, Tr. David Hinton

I

What Will Never Be

After the installation "All", by Maurizio Cattelan— Carrara marble sculptures of humans in body bags, exhibited in The Menil Collection in Houston, TX, 2010

These figures that we walk among aren't people.
    None of them has died or loved us,
        though we tend to think they have,

moving as we do through almost iridescent air-
    conditioned museum light while outside,
        Houston fumes with steam and summer rain.

We walk among nine staves of marble, figures sleeved
    in body bags, bend into them, but quietly, as if our air
        could wake them. It's awful in this city:

all the asphalt, heat we almost cannot bear.
    And we are awful, arguing over maps, laundering
        our underwear with shampoo in the motel sink.

But here in the museum, we stand so far apart
    you look anonymous, someone I love. Here is a body
        like the body I woke to this morning—slabs

of sunlight, bright as soap, from between the curtains—
    here its curl, left hip and shoulder sharp, spine turned
        in a gesture of embrace. And one I've covered

with a quilt—early spring, even the carpet cool
    back then in Massachusetts—torso flat and heavy,
        knees still cocked as if the figure means to rise.

And here it seems two bodies rest—
    knot of limbs, that heavy white material
        indecipherable—how many bodies lie here?

And the selves we don't inhabit anymore—
    are they nothing but their private suffering
        and pleasure? Stone is just a cold thing that we mine

and make a world of. Here I am, in Texas,
    in a summer overcome with rain. Across the room
        you're stoic in fluorescent light, hours since you've

touched me. The guard in the doorway, uniformed, yawning, watches
    either us or watches nothing. He's stunned, maybe, in this
        strange intimacy: what was, and what will never be.

In Spring
   —*After Li Bai*

Ponderosas dwarf you, towering over mesas there.
Forsythia froths along sidewalks here,
and tin cans, cellophane, neighbors' voices.
I got your letter yesterday—Utah, big trees,
thin beer, weird zip code—I love your open hand.
But I'd love anything from you. Why send me
just these empty blooms of scrawl? Say more.
Why strew me open, a mess of petals?

Postscript

I meant to write you more about the birds
and how they wake me, how near they seem
but aren't, as if those trills from almost invisible
sources thinned the distance between us.
I meant to seem familiar with my world,
enough to share it. But I had to look up
names; those words were only empty sounds—
warbler, waxwing, starling—that dilute.
Meanwhile, I taped your drawings to my fridge
as if to learn another language; your absence
stripped them down to glyphs. Please write.
Tell me where you are, to what you'd compare
these wings against the empty sky, or
this sense of what is neither here nor there.

Storm

Phlox breaking under rain
    all afternoon, skirts withered in puddles.
Pollen yellowed rivulets along the road.
    Such blinding rain, I had to feel my way
back home. Lizards busy the desert
    where you are, and cacti with their shameless,
sexual flowers. Evening here, my fingers
    count the days you've been away. I part
the curtains by my bed. Out front the oak,
    struck with such a brightness I stop breathing.
Parting my robe, I watch weather
    dismantle the yard, no one here to see me.
I watch dark in the split trunk widen. Soon,
    you say, you'll come home. Feel your way
through shocked dark into me. Won't you.

Pawnshop

Hung over this muralled desert city,
the moon wears the only face I've seen for hours.
It lights the pawnshop window,
orange poster board *closed* sign, my own face
in the glass while I stand eyeing the earrings.
It wears the mirth I used to search your face for
and not find. Last time I was here, I was with you.
We stole books and Dos Equis, screamed at each other
and drank by the arroyo. We tried on big-brimmed hats
and snuck sex in thrift store dressing rooms.
I followed your fast clip through the land
your father pocked with buried cash and arson
and he died in. Followed while the shape of you,
from far off, pierced the mesa. Years later
I've found little else I love. I'm see-through,
my right eye broken into by mourning
dove-shaped clip-ons made of Mexican silver.
My left cheek shot with red paste studs.
I would wear the beaded earrings with the image
of a phoenix rising through the image of my hair,
or the pair with horses draped in roses
printed on each ivory disk. Who would give up
that small pair, blossoms made of tear-shaped turquoise?
Who traded these in had to; she needed bus fare, flour.
The heart's deep pocket poverty struck,
one learns to give up what she loves.

Cliff Dwellings, Mesa Verde

What could we have found there,
awkward with our maps, silences,

grievances? Speechlessness was so
thick, thank god the red, parched road

wound up, starkly, so our breaths
thinned, and the dark, charred shrubs

along the carved-in mesa. I wanted
to be near you again, but you turned

to echoes from those shallow ruins
as ordered and homely as teeth.

How small they must have been.
I found only echoes—and the awful

closeness of people who aren't there.

II

Tinctures

Yarrow, she says, wading through the weeds
beside the mountain road, will purify the blood.

Gathering plants to make tinctures and balms,
serious and thinner now, my friend is learning

how to heal. Red clover lowers fever, quiets
frantic nerves. Stinging nettle soothes the skin,

the pain of aging joints. Saint John's wart, common
yellow flower, homely as a pillowcase, soothes the pain

of life itself. Well, pain has made a pagan of my friend.
Twenty-two, she's already learned to celebrate

death: friends, her father. Alone in her sugar shack home
up here, grown sinewy and stern, she studies the natural world

as if the names of living things, repeated, were a spell to undo loss.
She gives me what she gathers—hawthorn blossom, elder,

comfrey—to seal in jars with stones and alcohol. We're pulled over
here forever. The sun, once heavy gold with heat, is growing tired

over us, pale white light of evening setting in. Soon, she'll stop
and we'll start to enjoy what we always do together: at her place,

sepia sounds of guitar steeping from the record player, outside,
lake water steadying slowly under lowered sun. And we enjoy

the wine she makes: dandelion, lemon mint. Tasting of flowers
and of fire. Strong wine, and good, it puts us under fast.

Apples

All summer I tried to tell the need
for love from love. Now, October,

I see only how alone we grow,
discerning, combing through our harvest,

because I have been eating slowly
from the deep blue bowl of apples

on the table, so that now they bruise
themselves, are turning fragrant,

fogged with almost invisible flies.
But I think they were delicious.

Turns out what I love I can no longer have.

Aubade

Awake for hours, metal voiced, the neighbors' kids
        are outside, reestablishing obvious rules.
One seeks the others. My reawakened lover

yawns, his hardened cock against my thigh.
        Sun dampens the bed sheets. I don't know which
I want less: this man beside me, or that rising

chorus of laughs and defenses from kids,
        shrill with silly pleasures, who hide and taunt,
in whose rules to be touched is to lose.

North Street

Wind flustering my curtains with its gasoline
and pollen and the window of that bridal shop
have married in a sadness. Spring is relief
and struggle. Street musicians crooning
on the cinema steps down there must feel it too;
petals falling, gathering about them, beige
as aged lace. Sitting at an empty easel,
watching mountains turn to evening sky—
feels like this Joni Mitchell song in which she tries
to buy a mandolin but thinks about a wedding,
boats receding, someone dressing, someone
taking her own life, that kind of conversation.
I start to make some vows: to get more sleep,
head south again, play guitar, get outside more,
not to die alone. Through moving curtains:
ancient banks and lit-up storefronts, dim hills,
people still in t-shirts, playing, or just listening.

Dogwood

Effusions of blooms impossible
        to see beyond in June, bride-eager,
pulsing through the dark
        in which I sleep alone,
chastened in the dormer's origami.

Dust flocks the floorboards;
        my foot prints shine on oak.
Outside, tufts of flowers aloft
        in fleeting swoons—spectacles
of lace and beads of stamen.

Up close, each flower
        more green than white,
more leaf than petal, eyelid-soft,
        bright-edged as a star.
I've come to need the tree

to be this—object
        I don't understand
and cannot take my eyes from
        so that, waking after rain to birds'
absurd hyperbole, I saw the branches

flowerless again and drowsed
        down to the floor by the window
to gather the spume of petals
        strewn into the room.
How strange

that they weren't flowers
        but were several slight, white moths,
upturned and dry as pages,
        powdered wings so fragile
they dissolved at my most careful touch.

III

Nest

Erupting from the barn,

relief of birds against blue.

Off now together in a fluster

I interpret as affection. Recollect

the nest I left at home, blanching

in its crook of oak. Tatted thing—

whorled grass and tinsel; crimps

of undone tarpaulin hung down.

Slight home, spun and silent.

Still another world I couldn't enter.

Fall

My mother's yard, pears sunk into the ground
under the gray tree. Fall coming, day going: commerce
of light and other light; fruit striking the ground. I laid myself

down in the grass, in the shade, where the fallen
pears softened and broke, their bruises swooning with flies.
I lay, and broke into something like sleep.

My mother fears flesh the way some fear death.
Like the body is ruled by the wound that ruins it.
Not far, inside, her voice, a struck wire,

called to me. I stayed out there alone, though,
while the ground grew hard, her voice grew far as metal.

My Mother's Patent Leather Pumps

She kept them stuffed with tissue
in the box she'd bought them in—
teal, its sixties ribbony script
impossible to parse. But I know
what these mean to her by now;

she gave them to me. Wearing
her best shoes to dinner, say, or
on a holiday, they're stiff as treasure
still, and shine, and we are lustrous,
untouched by age, contained, and aching.

Elegy For My Mother's Dress

Where is it now, the dress my mother asks to be buried in?
Floor length, A-line, narrow as a knife, she wore it to the wedding

that she didn't eat at forty years ago, then once to the theater.
She can find neither the dress now nor the photos of her in it;

crouched, lumbering though the attic, sweat spangles her brow.
But she used to show them to me often—photographs

of her, reposed, wearing the black and white sheath—
so the garment is inarched with my idea of what she was

before she snapped last time: brittle, pretty and abysmal.
Her body was a sleeve she shrunk from once, now swells beyond.

No doubt the dress won't fit her anymore.
But let's not doubt for a minute

that my mother, damp in her stretched-out t-shirt, breathing hard
in glowing dust, still has decades left to look for it.

If, she instructs, it doesn't fit her when she dies,
I should drape it, graphic and flat as a flag, over her closed coffin.

Closing my eyes as if, blinded, I might find it,
I can almost smell the fabric, stiff with must and Shalimar.

I can almost see what she says she fears: see the moths—
a flurry of hunger and bone white wings—

envelop the dress, then eat it thread by thread.

Lilacs

Where hung clusters,
        heavy, bee-dusted, whose
fragrance stunned memory
        to ache, now dust-colored
blooms gone airy as ash
        remind it's ache I love.

This yard a sprawl I've walked
        and walked, as if the past were
perfume I could breathe of,
        so the present is worried
as tatted lace, frayed,
        yellowing. Mid-summer,

mid-day, my mother sleeps
        in her lavender muumuu;
snug, its pearl snaps tugged
        to zigzag. Glistening
on the lawn divan, she is
        a kind of blossom too,

the air of her alive with talcum
        and sweet sweat. Flower-stitched,
a pink mule dangles from her ankle.
        What isn't a world? A garden?
Where isn't everything growing
        still, invisible, persistent? Piled

fashion magazines beside her gleam
  and slide like platelets shifting;
perfumed pages, torn out, gummed,
  come apart in heat. The only movement
hot breeze and her deep, accordionic
  breathing. Lilacs burned

this year before I got here. Still
  I can almost taste their air
that aches and stays the heart.
  Papery and blank, they stand,
I like to think, for nothing. But
  in bloom, they rouse a question

I was born with and can't answer.
  I watch my mother sleep
for minutes before waking her.
  How many afternoons like this.
I recollect the lilacs, thinking
  why what I love troubles me.

The Garden

Something's gone to seed;
>seeds remove themselves
and hover, incandescent

as the dead. In her garden,
>in rough, accustomed sun
that tires the chard, my friend

works. I lie out here, burn taut
>as hide, urging my skin to age,
watching it darken. Beside me,

among the anonymous greens,
>her bent head, red as a flare,
regards me, concerned.

From time to time a breeze comes,
>or a helicopter chortles overhead.
When I wanted to be dead

I worked to keep it to myself,
>and helped string up that chaos
of tomatoes: cherry, brandywine.

I worked, stitched myself to this earth
>of hers as it were the only world.
My friend said I was good at it.

>She thanked me.

Emily Pulfer-Terino is a poet and writer whose work has appeared in *Tupelo Quarterly, Hunger Mountain, The Southeast Review, Poetry Northwest, Stone Canoe, The Louisville Review, Juked,* and other journals and anthologies. She has been a Tennessee Williams Poetry Scholar at the Sewanee Writer's Conference and has been granted a fellowship for creative non-fiction at the Vermont Studio Center. She holds an MFA in creative writing from Syracuse University, and she lives in Western Massachusetts.

www.ingramcontent.com/pod-product-compliance
Lightning Source LLC
Chambersburg PA
CBHW060226050426
42446CB00013B/3185